Diana,

Che
a frui
2017 brings you happiness &
prosperity.

PRISON TO PROMISED LAND

It's Not Over Until We Die

by Zachary Babcock

To My Mother
Gail Flier Babcock

Without you I wouldn't be who I am today.
You never once stopped believing in me
throughout your life.
Always so quick to give and slow to take.
You showed me how to love and that it
matters the most.
And you inspired everyone around you to be
more.

Dedication

Stephanie, my wife and my rock, you give me love and encouragement when I need it the most, and you've blessed me with a beautiful family.

Landon and Liam, I love you, boys. My greatest wishes for when you grow up are that you never give up on yourselves and that you pursue your dreams and purposes as if your lives depend on it.

Isabella, although you are my stepdaughter, I love you as though you are my own. You make me smile every day. I want you to have everything your heart desires.

John, your story is inspiring, and your no-surrender attitude motivates me every day.

Christian, Joe, and Dwayne, you inspired me to write this book now instead of later.

Table of Contents

Chapter 1
Life Leading up to Prison

I come from a very entrepreneurial family. My maternal grandfather was a great car salesman and started his own successful dealership. My father was their top used car salesman for many years. My mother and father met at the dealership. They were married a few years later.

I grew up in Wildwood, Missouri, with my mother, father, and my older sister, Meghan. We had a close and functional family. It seemed like there was never a dull moment.

My mother and father's marriage didn't last. After they divorced when I was six,

Meghan and I lived with our mother full time and stayed with our father every other weekend. My mother was working two jobs, trying to keep up with the house payments, until we moved to Ferguson, Missouri, shortly after my parents divorced.

Ferguson is a beautiful town. I despise how the media hypes it up to be some horrible place. We are a great town with many great citizens who go above and beyond to make it a great community. Many wonderful organizations have been created here, dedicated to giving back to our city to make it an exceptional place to live.

Shortly after we moved to Ferguson, my father was killed in a car accident. I was seven. I never cried when he passed—not because I didn't love him, but I guess because I was too young to understand what that really meant.

I give my mother all the praise in the

world for being so strong and doing the best any single mother could do to raise two children on her own. She was well known, loved, and respected in the Ferguson community for her selfless acts to improve it as a whole. My mother told me every day that I could do anything I put my mind to. I have no doubt that I am where I am today because of her unconditional love and belief in me.

Back then I was a knucklehead, to put it mildly. I didn't have a father figure in my life anymore, and I started making poor decisions. I began to look up at my older sister's guy friends as role models who I thought were cool. I started skipping school, smoking weed, and getting into fights with other kids because I thought it was cool at that time.

Over the next few years, I was in and out of juvenile detention centers and group homes. I was the kid who completely refused to go to school in the fourth grade, and I would purposely get into trouble when I was forced to go. I wasn't stupid, by any means, but I just didn't have the attention span to sit in a class unless the subject interested me. Nothing in school held my interest. I was put on probation through Saint Louis County Family Courts for truancy from school, and then I started failing drug tests for weed.

Eminem was my idol from age twelve through sixteen. Four friends and I decided to start a rap group. We were young and extremely passionate about music. We made CDs, performed at local venues in Saint Louis, opened for Chingy, a famous Saint Louis rapper, and participated in the Vibe Music Fest Contest in Atlanta, Georgia, in June of 2005.

When we quit making music together in 2006, I really started making horrible decisions. At this point, I started my first sales job at seventeen and fell in love with it. A people person, I love to connect with other people and take a genuine interest in them. I worked as a door-to-door canvasser for a company. My job was to relate to people, figure out their needs, and then show them how our company could solve their problems. I would set up consultations for a sales representative to come out to their house and lock in a contract for either thermal windows, siding, roofing, or gutters. A sale takes place when need meets opportunity, and I was a natural. I really loved my work.

However, I was also seventeen and still wanted to be cool, so I started selling all different kinds of illegal drugs. That quickly escalated to using these drugs as well. I started burglarizing homes, and before I even knew what hit me, I was a full-blown drug addict. I remember smoking crack cocaine with people in run-down motel rooms and searching the carpet for nonexistent crack crumbs after our dope was gone. I remember shooting heroin into my arm and overdosing at a friend's house. I woke to him slapping me in the face while he was holding me, fully clothed, in a cold shower. I could have died and would have had he not put me in that cold shower.

Countless times, I woke up with no money, dope sick because my body was dependent on heroin. I had hot and cold flashes, sweating out of control, extreme pain in my lower back, and stomachaches out of this world. I would get together with my dope buddies, and we would steal anything we could get our hands on. I was out there bad.

Shortly after my near-death experience, I got sentenced to seven years in the Missouri Department of Corrections on April 28, 2008. At nineteen, I was a convicted felon with absolutely no direction in life. But I was cool.

Chapter 2
Welcome to the Joint

I would serve the next four years of my life in prison, but first there was the anticipation. Not a clue about where I was going in life. All I knew was that I had screwed up big time, and now I was going to pay for it. This was the first time I'd ever felt powerless.

In the back of my mind, I always knew that I was going to be someone and that I could do whatever I put my mind to. My mother gave me that confidence in myself from day one. Yet I had absolutely no idea what I was going to do at this time. I was worried about just making it out of prison.

Let me clear this up now. Yes, prison is a horrible place to be. Most of the people in prison are the scum of the earth. Yes, I did fight a few times during my stay, mainly in the early days when the other convicts were testing me to see if I would stand up for myself, but it was not as scary as I thought it was going to be.

I sat in Saint Louis County Jail for six months, waiting as my court date kept being continued. During this time, all I would think about all day long was getting covered in tattoos and getting in tip-top shape. Nervous about going to prison, I thought I was going to have to fight for my life like in the movies and TV shows.

On October 1, 2008, I made it into prison, exactly one day after I turned twenty. Sure enough, I killed my time by working ou and getting tattoos. In jail, I would go to slee at night visualizing what I would look like in amazing physical condition and laid out with some dope tattoos. That was exactly how it ended up going. It's funny how we become what we think about the most.

After about a year of being incarcerated, my time started to speed up. By this time, I was familiar with how everything operated in prison, and I had developed a daily routine that kept me busy and my mind off home.

As I mentioned, I proceeded to get covered in tattoos, which also resulted in me spending significant time in the hole, the prison inside of prison. The hole at this particular prison had eight-by-ten cells where we were either by ourselves or had one cellmate, our celly.

We got three measly and disgusting meals a day served to us through a chuckhole in our cell door. Even though the food was horrible, our options were to man up and eat it or to go hungry. Being hungry is one of the worst feelings in the world to me, so I opted to man up.

We were allowed to have three optional five-minute showers a week. Yes, I said three showers a week, and yes, I said optional. Believe it or not, there were guys in there who were flat-out nasty. They didn't clean themselves or their living space. We called them Vikings.

We got mail Monday through Friday, and we were allowed to have three books in our cell. Those books were so old and boring that they either put you right to sleep or gave you tunnel vision trying to focus on the words.

I had to do two months in the hole for my fifth tattoo violation. About a week into my stay, a correctional officer (CO for short) banged on my door and said, "You Babcock?"

My response was very disrespectful with

explicit words.

He told me to cuff up because I was going to the captain's office.

Immediately, I thought I was being put under investigation for all the things I didn't get caught doing on the main prison yard, like gambling in poker and spades games and writing tickets for people who wanted to gamble on professional sporting events. I told the CO that I didn't have anything to say, but he took me anyway.

Two COs escorted me to the captain's office in shackles and handcuffs. When I arrived, the captain said, "Mr. Babcock, how long have you been locked up now?"

At twenty-one, I had been incarcerated for over two years, so I rudely answered, "Two years."

"Mr. Babcock, you know by now that anytime someone gets called to my office, it isn't good news."

I said, "I don't care, man! I get out of the hole in two months. I don't have anything to say. Write me a violation if you want. I don't know anything."

"Mr. Babcock, we received a call over the weekend from your mother. Your sister passed away from a heroin overdose."

I went into shock. First, my vision blacked out for a few seconds, and I became extremely dizzy. Then the tears started to pour out, and I couldn't put my words together.

After being escorted to the phone cage, I was allowed a thirty-second phone call. My mother was absolutely devastated. What mother wouldn't be? She told me that she'd had to pry the bathroom door open with a screwdriver to find my sister dead with a needle in her arm. We were both crying uncontrollably, and all I could keep saying was "I'm sorry" over and over. The phone automatically hung up before I could tell my mother that I loved her.

I felt big enough to sit on a penny and swing my feet from it. I just wanted to be there for her, and here I was, unable to talk to her for another two months because I was in the hole for being stupid.

Not in the right frame of mind for a celly, I told the COs that I needed to be put in a single cell. Thankfully, they accepted my request. Normally, they don't care about the inmates or their feelings.

In my single cell, I cried my heart out that night and the next few days. It was miserable. I was in a cell, isolated from all human interaction. All I could think about was my sister and my mother. I didn't eat. I didn't even want to get out of my bunk. I lay there for most of the day but occasionally got up to pace my tiny cell.

My sister was a sweet and beautiful girl,

and she always had my back. She could have done anything she set her heart to. Instead, she got involved with the wrong crowd and made poor decisions.

My mother went on to create an organization in the Ferguson community called Ferguson Youth Initiative, FYI, in honor of Meghan's memory. FYI has great people come in and mentor the Ferguson youth who have gotten into some kind of trouble in school or with the law. They let the youth participate in 5K runs held by the city, and they have concerts in which the youth participate by performing music or dancing. The youth contribute to all kinds of art displays at these concerts.

My mother also lobbied for Ferguson to enact a law that the youth be given the option to do community service work to beautify the city instead of paying a ticket for something minor, like speeding. This is genius, because most of those kids can't pay those tickets and end up getting into more trouble because of it. Ferguson was the first municipality in the US to implement this.

While she was honoring my sister, I started going crazy from being in the hole, coping with the loss of my sister with virtually no human contact. I had to develop a routine to keep me sane and to pass my time. I would wake up for breakfast, then go back to sleep. I would then wake up for the rest of the day about an hour before lunch. I would start my day by lying there praying and meditating. Then I would get up, brush my teeth, and wash my face. After that, I would stand at my door and wait for the COs to come around with lunch. After lunch, I would lie on my back and read a book for about an hour to let my food digest.

Then I got creative. In the hole, we were allowed two bath towels that we could wash once a week. I ripped up one of my towels into a bunch of small rags, each one for a specific purpose. I would flip my mat in half on my bunk, then grab all of my personal property and set it down on the other side of the bunk. Then I would use one of my mini-rags with soap to scrub the walls, another rag to scrub my sink, and another rag to scrub the toilet. After that, I would sweep the floor with my bare hand and gather up all of the dirt and dust bunnies into a pile. Using your hand to sweep, you will pick up a lot more dust than using a broom, but it does take you a lot longer. To get all of the dust up, I would ball up a few squares of toilet paper and dampen it in the sink, then I would mash the damp toilet paper down on the dust to pick up every spot. Finally, I would use another mini-rag to scrub the floor with soap. That process would take me about an hour and a half every day. It was a great way to pass my time and keep my cell spotless.

After I finished cleaning, I would exercise until dinner was served. I developed a cell workout that consisted of five hundred each of regular push-ups, incline push-ups, squats, sit-ups, crunches, leg raises, shoulder rotations to the front, and shoulder rotations to the back. Then, every other day I would do ten sets of twenty burpees. You won't get big on this regime, but you will definitely get shredded.

Dinner would be served about fifteen minutes after I completed my workout. I would read on my back in my bunk for another thirty minutes to an hour after dinner to let my food digest. Then I would pace back and forth for an hour or two, just to move around and think, until the COs came around to pass out the mail. I responded to any mail I received. If I didn't receive any mail, I would look at my address book and write a letter to someone I hadn't heard from in a while.

Then it was time to wind down for the night and do it all over again for the next two months. That was the only way I could keep my sanity while being contained in a tiny living space with minimal human interaction.

~~~

About three weeks after my sister passed away, something amazing happened. I had some kind of spiritual awakening. I really don't know how to explain it other than I had some inner voice inside me that put me at peace with the universe. I knew everything was happening exactly how it was supposed to and everything was going to be okay. I didn't know how; I just had that gut feeling, and it felt good.

I started to look at the world differently. I started being grateful that I had three meals a day and shelter. This carried on with me after I was placed back into a regular housing unit on the main yard.

For the most part, everyone always looked for something to be negative about.

"It's too hot outside."

"We should have air conditioning in our housing unit."

"These COs are too petty."

However, there are a few people in there with good hearts and good intentions.

I started observing the world around me in a new light, with gratitude. I was grateful for everything. Perhaps I was trapped inside a barbwire fence guarded by COs with firearms and secluded away from home and all of my family and friends, yet I was at peace with myself. I realized this was part of the process of my journey and that I was completely responsible for the rest of my life and all of its outcomes.

For the next two years, I continued with my normal routine to pass my time. I stayed out of trouble for the most part, and my time seemed to fly by.

I matured a lot in prison and developed character that I would not have developed any other way. I am forever grateful for my stay in prison. Without it, I wouldn't be the man I am today.

Chapter 3
Home Sweet Home

After serving four years flat on a seven-year sentence, I was released from prison on February 28, 2012, into society with three years of parole to walk down. I can't even describe in words the level of euphoria I felt as I stepped into the free world.

The prison was located forty-five minutes from our home in Ferguson, so my mother was there to pick me up. She brought an outfit that I had to change into before I left the prison—an outfit that I had prior to being incarcerated.

Now remember, I was incarcerated at the very beginning of 2008. It was now 2012, and a lot of things changed in the world over the course of those four years, including clothing styles. To make matters worse, I was a wannabe thug before prison, and I wore clothes that could fit Sasquatch!

I remember putting on the size 44 jeans that my mother brought from home, knowing that my real size was 32, and looking desperately at my mother. "Ma, I know that I am a grown man and that I have to take care of myself, but would it be okay if we go find a pair of jeans that fit me?" She just busted out laughing, more than happy to help me.

We went to Target to get some jeans, and I remember feeling so much anxiety walking into the store among normal people. It was extremely weird and uncomfortable for me. I couldn't understand why everyone was so friendly and why people were smiling so much. I thought everyone was watching my every move and that if I touched anything in that store, I would be accused of stealing and thrown back in prison.

Interacting with a female employee there was also extremely uncomfortable. For the past four years, I had been around men, for the most part. It was just plain weird.

After we found a pair of jeans, I asked my mother if I could go wait in the car while she stood in line to pay for the jeans because I felt freaked out. She laughed and handed me the keys, and I was out of there fast.

In this Target store, they had automatic sliding glass doors to enter on one side and to exit on the other. In between these doors was a middle section of doors and space to store the shopping carts. There weren't any shopping carts in this area at the time, and I thought it was just another passageway to get in and out of the store, so I elected to take these doors because too many people for my liking were using the other two doors.

The doors did not slide open for me. By this point, I was having a nervous breakdown. I thought the employees had locked the doors and were sending the police to come get me. Eventually, I found the proper exit, and we made it out with a pair of jeans that fit me.

At first, it was extremely difficult for me to adjust to this new world. I remember asking to use my friend Andrew's phone to call another friend and then not knowing how to use the new smartphone he handed me. I could not wrap my brain around the fact that I did not know how to make a phone call. I didn't get it. And being around women who were not COs and communicating with them was just weird and awkward for me for the first few weeks.

With consistent effort and belief, I slowly but surely adjusted to the real world. About a month after getting out, I landed a job as a cook at a bar and grill up the street from our home in Ferguson. Then I got another job at another bar and grill close to our home as a cook because there were more hours available for me to work.

A lot of my friends came to this bar often, and here I was, brand new to the bar scene at twenty-three. I began to party a lot and drink socially. When I say "party," I mean we would close down the bar, then go over to East Saint Louis where clubs didn't close. I continued to work at the bar and grill fifty to sixty hours a week and party there every night. I was extremely motivated in life, but I was also trying to make up for lost time.

I learned the hard way that you can't make up for lost time.

One night when it was only the cool kitchen manager and me working, this drop-dead beautiful brunette with green eyes and tattoos came into the already packed bar in a stunning white dress. I don't know if it was her looks, the wing tattoo on her back, or the white dress that blew me away, or if it was a combination of all of these factors. I just couldn't keep my eyes off her. I was supposed to be doing the dishes, but I was distracted.

She was with a guy. I didn't know if this guy was her boyfriend or not, but I figured he was by their body language. Why would a beautiful woman like her be single?

I didn't care that she was with him. In my mind, she was already with me; she just didn't know it yet. I was dead set, and there wasn't anything that anyone could have told me otherwise.

When we slowed down in the kitchen, I made my move. My exact words to my manager as I was leaving the kitchen were, "I'm going in."

I walked right up to her and her

boyfriend, told her how beautiful she was, and asked her why I'd never seen her before. Of course, she rejected me and walked away with her boyfriend. I told her, "I'll see you again."

Sure enough, a few weeks later, while I was at work, one of the bartenders was training a new employee. The new bartender was the woman in the white dress.

At this point, it was only a matter of time before she would be with me, so I just played it cool and got to know her through work. We would hang out together after shifts at the bar with other coworkers, but that was it.

Then one night, I had just finished my shift and was hanging out on the huge deck with two of my friends. She sat about five tables down from us with a bunch of her friends. I kept shooting her looks, and she kept returning them. Finally she walked over to our table and started talking to me but was quickly interrupted when a friend from the neighborhood was being kicked out of the bar for being extremely intoxicated.

He was screaming insults at the top of his lungs and started ripping signs off the walls and hitting the deck. I don't know why I felt obligated to help protect the bar, but I did. I jumped over the deck to tell him to stop, to go home and sleep it off. Of course, a belligerently intoxicated man isn't going to listen to that, and the situation quickly escalated into a physical fight.

While I had him in a choke hold, I saw cop cars pull up and police officers jump out. I immediately let go, and he was hit with the Taser. They took him to jail and placed handcuffs on me. My boss told them I was in the clear, and I was let out of the handcuffs.

When I went back into the bar, my two friends told me that it looked like the Taser was intended for me, as it looked like I was the aggressor in the conflict, and that I released the choke hold just in time. Lucky me.

So the girl that I couldn't stop thinking about for the past month came over and asked if I wanted to go with her and three of her girlfriends to the casino. Now it was my turn to decline. I told her I didn't want to leave my two friends there at the bar.

The next day, July 8, 2012, we started dating, and today she is my wife. Stephanie is the love of my life and my rock.

For the next eight months, I continued to work at the bar and grill and party there after work, but not as much now that I was dating Stephanie.

There was a clothing store that I was obsessed with and shopped at all the time. I walked in there one day, clothed in their expensive merchandise from head to toe, and was interested in one of their displays.

The store manager walked over and said, "May I help you with something?"

I responded, "Yes, how much is it for that mannequin?"

"What item are you talking about? The outer shirt, the undershirt, the—"

"How much for everything on the mannequin?"

He looked at me and asked, "Have you ever worked here before?"

"No, but I would love to."

The next day I got the job on the spot. I was stoked! I landed a job in sales at a store where I loved to shop for clothes! That meant I got to help people find what they wanted, and I got 40 percent off all merchandise! WIN-WIN!

Two weeks into my new sales job, I was promoted into management. One day during my first week, I sold over $3,000 in merchandise on a six-hour shift, and the store closed that day at just over $9,000. My sales were one-third of the entire operation that day.

I was beyond excited and put in my two-weeks' notice at the bar and grill where I had been working fifty to sixty hours a week for the past ten months. I was moving on and moving up. Things were really starting to come together for me, and I couldn't be happier.

Two days after I put my notice in at the bar and grill, I was called into the office at my sales job for a phone conference with my store manager and human resources in corporate. They told me that my promotion had caused a red flag in their system because I was a convicted felon. They had to let me go.

So here I was, all excited about making a huge upgrade in my career, only to find out now that I didn't have a job at all. I went from working fifty to sixty hours a week with stability in my life to nothing.

I was crushed. Instead of looking at all of my options and staying positive, I decided to throw a pity party. Fear and doubt began to creep into my mind. My thoughts were that my conviction record was going to hinder me from ever living a decent life and that I would never be able to live my dreams.

This was when my drinking became a problem. I started hanging out with a friend I grew up with in Ferguson, and all we did was drink and party. All day, every day.

I ended up getting a job selling steaks door to door out the back of a pickup truck. I probably could have done very well at this job, but I just didn't care because I was feeling sorry for myself and had become an alcoholic. I cared more about drinking than I did about mastering my sales pitch and dealing with resistance. I lasted only a few weeks at that job.

Then Stephanie informed me that she was pregnant. I started drinking even more, trying my hardest to escape the reality of everything happening in my life. I worked a lot of different side jobs that paid cash but nothing steady.

Then while we were at the hospital, the nurse informed us that we were having twins. I almost fainted right there in the room. I was shell-shocked. I was about to be responsible for three children, and I didn't know how I was going to be able to provide for them. I had Stephanie, my stepdaughter Isabella, and twin babies to take care of now. I thought, *How can I take care of my family when I can't even take care of myself?*

I started drinking more than ever. I realized that the only way for me to ever get ahead and have any kind of decent life was to work for myself. The only problem was that I had no idea how I was going to do that.

A friend and I had T-shirts printed up that said, "Zero Fucks Are Given." This was the friend that I was partying with all the time, and we were complete idiots. We began to sell these T-shirts all over Saint Louis through our friends, social media, and random people. I would have the people who bought a shirt take a photo of them in the T-shirt with me, then post it on Facebook and tag them in it. This would then pop up on all of my friends' news feeds on Facebook as well as all of their friends' and really helped generate more sales.

For two alcoholics, we did a good job of selling shirts. We would move 150–200 shirts in a few days at $10 a shirt while we paid $2–$3 per shirt. The only problem was that we would keep enough money to purchase more shirts, then go party with the rest. At this time, I was being a complete alcoholic scumbag, and I was cheating on Stephanie with several girls.

I got an idea to host a rap concert at a venue in Saint Louis. I used to perform in shows all the time when I was with my rap group, but I had never hosted one before. I found a venue and set a date for the concert. I lined up eleven artists and groups to perform at the concert and gave each of them twenty-five tickets for $125 so they could turn around and sell each ticket for $10 and make $125 for themselves. I found a bouncer for the front door, and I charged $15 at the door, which the bouncer and I split fifty-fifty. Then my party buddy and another friend set up a table to sell our shirts.

We had a huge turnout. Pretty much everyone we knew was at this show. After all was said and done, I made $1,300 in profit that night . . . and I blew it all.

We put together another show. By this time I was cheating on Stephanie with a woman I grew up with in Ferguson. This girl had started using heroin, and I started using it as well when I would go see her. I was being a complete scumbag in all areas of my life, and I really didn't care.

We did our second show, and I made a little over a grand this time. I went to stay with the other woman and pretty much blew all of the money on heroin.

I woke up the next day, dope sick for the first time in years. I couldn't believe I had let myself go to this again after losing my sister to heroin. I knew heroin leads you down only two roads: jail or death. I made the decisions right then and there, dope sick and all, that I wasn't going to do this again and that I couldn't live like this anymore.

I bought a pint of E&J liquor to knock the edge off my withdrawal and kept it in my coat pocket all day to sip on often. I was absolutely miserable, but I wasn't going to go back to that old lifestyle. I made it through the heroin withdrawal, and after four days, I was back to normal. I had successfully quit using heroin on my own, but I was still drinking like it was going out of style.

One night I got a DWI. When I was pulled over, I refused to take a breath test, so I was taken into custody. I bonded out and contacted my parole officer right away to inform him what had happened. He told me that I was not going to be sent back to prison for this DWI but that I needed to get it taken care of.

I ended up getting a job at a restaurant as a cook. That only lasted about three weeks. I literally felt like a slave when I was there. I don't like being bossed around and being told when I can use the bathroom, when I can or cannot sit down, and so on. I've never been good with following the rules anyway. That ended up being the last time I would trade my time for money.

About a month after I got fired from the restaurant, I was at a local bar in Ferguson. I ended up getting blackout drunk, and the police were called because I was trying to fight a friend. I still have no recollection of this.

I woke up in the Ferguson jail to learn that I had a parole hold on me and that I was heading back to prison for six months or until I finished my sentence in fifteen months. This was twenty days before my sons were born.

Can you imagine waking up from a blackout drunk in jail and learning that you are about to go back to prison and will miss your sons being born all because you felt sorry for yourself and chose to party? That feeling was unbearable. That was the lowest I'd ever felt in my life. I'd let down my entir family and myself.

That was the defining moment in my life. That was when I became a man. I decided right there in my cell that I was never going to feel sorry for myself again and that I was completely responsible for my circumstances. Mistakes and bad conditions or successes and blessings didn't matter; it was all my responsibility and my doing.

I told myself that I was going to go do whatever time I had to do and then be done with that life for good. I was going to come home and be the man I knew I could be.

Chapter 4
A New Man

I didn't blame anyone or anything but myself for my circumstances. I took full responsibility for landing myself back in prison. I knew it was completely up to me to get out and live the life I desired.

My sons, Landon James Babcock and Liam Denis Babcock, were born on February 20, 2014, and they gave my life new meaning. I was crushed that I couldn't be there when they were born, but I finally understood that it was time for me to man up. It wasn't about me anymore. It was about my family. I never had a father figure growing up, and I wasn't about to let Landon and

Liam not have one either.

A few weeks after my sons were born, I found out that Stephanie had started dating someone else. This someone else happened to be the father of my other woman's child. When I found out that I was going back to prison, I expected her to see someone else, since that's what usually happens in these cases. After what I put her through, I really couldn't blame her. However, her getting with the guy who had a baby with the girl I cheated on her with really bothered me.

I was really upset, but I couldn't do anything about it except to do my time and get back home. I just had to accept that fact and focus on myself, on how I could be an asset to my sons.

When I was transferred to a mainline camp about an hour and a half away from home, I was able to get a visit. I held my sons for the first time on June 22, 2014. My heart melted the moment I laid eyes on them, and I fell in love right away. I was more determined than ever to put that old lifestyle behind me.

A few weeks after that, on the Fourth of July weekend, I called home and found out my smaller boy, Landon, had been rushed to the hospital because his head was swollen. He had a fractured skull and brain hemorrhaging. Stephanie and my mother told me that the hospital and child services wanted to investigate the situation further. They believed that Landon could have been hit by someone.

I immediately told Stephanie that the guy she was seeing had hurt my son, but she didn't believe it and stood up for him. I knew it was him right away. Anytime I get a strong gut feeling like that, it is always true. Plus, it made sense if his girlfriend, the mother of his child, was cheating on him with me. I guess i wasn't good enough for him to hook up with

Stephanie, so he fractured my four-month-old infant son's head.

Sure enough, they took my sons into custody. During the police investigation, he confessed that he had hit my son.

I was so worried for my son. I didn't want him to have brain damage or be messed up for the rest of his life because some coward was mad at me and hit him. At the same time, I had never had so much hate for one person in my life. Thank God I was locked up at the time because there isn't any telling what I might have done to that scumbag when I found this out.

Stephanie ended up getting back custody of our children, and she was confident that they were going to send the guy to prison. I told her that he belonged in prison, but he would get a slap on the wrist and probation.

See, the justice system here in Missouri is a joke. The government officials should be ashamed of themselves. You see this time and again: Guys like me who have burglarized houses, stolen cars, assaulted law enforcement officers, and escaped from custody absolutely deserve to do four years on a seven-year sentence. But how do you justify grown men who physically harm little children only getting a slap on the wrist with as little as a two- or three-year sentence and then only have to pull six or eight months on it before they get right back out on the streets? Some only get probation and no time. There isn't any justice in that at all. These sexual predators and child abusers are scarring innocent children for life, and they barely have to pay any price for it. That's a huge problem, if you ask me, and I hope it is addressed immediately.

The next few months were very humbling for me. I realized that if I did go after this coward when I got out, it would only hurt my family and take me away from them again. That was not an option for me. I had to deal with it and have faith that the universe would take care of the process. That was extremely hard and humbling for me. In the end, my family means the most to me, and I am going to always do what is best for them.

The last few months in prison seemed to drag on. The family courts ruled against letting my sons come up to visit me in prison, and that was driving me crazy. That didn't make any sense at all to me. I have never had any incident with any kind of child endangerment in my life. I couldn't wrap my mind around the fact that the courts ruled against me seeing my sons when I hadn't done anything for them to make that judgment.

On October 2, 2014, I was released from prison with seven months left on parole. It was different this time. I didn't know exactly what I was going to do, but I knew I was going to do whatever it took to take care of my family.

The family courts did not allow me to see my sons except for one two-hour supervised visit a week. I didn't follow that directive. I've never been good at following the rules anyway. I thought it was ridiculous and spent hours with my sons every single day. My thought process was that they were trying to take a good father from his children when he had already served his time for something that had nothing to do with the children. I felt like I was getting double jeopardy.

So here I was, a twenty-six-year-old man, fresh out of prison, coming home to eight-month-old twin sons. I had bills to pay, no job, no money, and no idea of what I wanted to do or how to move forward. I just had a burning desire to provide for my family and be someone.

I started looking for jobs right away. I filled out applications everywhere with no luck. Every single day, I was hunting for opportunities that seemed at the time completely out of reach. I quit filling out applications online because I knew that I didn't stand a chance as a convicted felon. Instead, I went into businesses and filled out applications in person. Still no luck.

A month and a half later, something amazing happened. I hit the gym five or six times a week, and I would post photos on Instagram with hashtags related to health and fitness so other people could view my posts and account.

Some guy I didn't know commented on one of my posts. He asked me if I wanted to try a drink. I didn't know him or this drink, but I told him I'd like to know if I could make any money with it. He told me, yes, I could, and he happened to live ten minutes from me. So we set up a time to meet and go over all of the details.

I met up with him and his business partner at a restaurant, sampled the product, and was shown the business opportunity. I loved the product. It was an all-natural, plant-based supplement that I could get really excited about. I quickly realized that I could replace a few products that I was already using with these products that were healthier for me and less expensive. And I could get paid for building a business with them. WIN-WIN!

In order for me to make money in this business, I had to purchase products every month to consume myself and to share with other people. The only way to earn money was to build my own organization of customers and other distributors. I'd never heard of something like this before, but I was super excited about it. Creating and building an organization from nothing sounded so cool to me, right up my alley.

The minimum monthly package to qualify to earn commissions required an investment of $125 to $150. I didn't have a dime to my name, but I looked them in the eye and said I would be back in two days to place my order and join the team.

I talked with my mother and explained everything to her. She told me that I was looking at a network marketing company. She also praised the industry and told me that she and my father did network marketing before I was born. They loved the industry.

I was very blessed that my mother and Stephanie believed in me and helped me purchase my products for the first three months until my business became profitable. I didn't make a single commission check my first five weeks as I started learning how to build the business. I had great mentors who showed me how to be a network marketing professional and walked me through every step. They continue to mentor me today. That is so huge because I believe wholeheartedly that I wouldn't be where I am today without the mentorship I received from my team.

That's why I love this industry: it is all about helping people in four basic ways. First, my company, Xango, is a health and wellness company with superior health and wellness products. So we help people experience better health with our products. I was using a pre-workout product that was very bad for my health, but now I take products that are great for my health.

The second way we help people is by offering business opportunities. For those who are looking for additional income or want to build up enough income to replace their current job and work from the comfort of their own home, we help them do just that if they have what it takes. This industry can give you time freedom and financial freedom if you treat it like a real business and work it as if your life depends on it. It takes a strong individual with a significant reason to build this business. It isn't for everyone because, quite frankly, most people are whiners, crybabies, and excuse-makers who simply will not do the simple things necessary to build a network marketing business.

The third way we help people is through personal development. We set goals, show people how to set goals, hold each other accountable, have training in a wide variety of subjects, and encourage daily reading. Before joining this industry, I never read books daily or wrote down my goals. I've grown so much from this experience, and I wouldn't have grown the way I have without the mentors I have.

The fourth way we help people is by feeding hungry mouths all around the world. A percentage of every single sale that takes place in my company goes to feed starving children and nursing mothers in over twenty countries worldwide. Our team has even set up donation boxes for change in local businesses, which goes to feeding the needy. I used to be unable to take care of myself, and now I'm helping feed people in third world countries.

After five weeks of talking to everyone I could think of about my product, my story, and my opportunity, I signed up the first distributor in my organization. I met him through Instagram. He is a very sharp man from New Bedford, Massachusetts.

After that, I went on a tear. People started joining my business left and right. The people who joined me started duplicating what I was doing. My business was growing rapidly when just a few months prior, I had been sitting in prison unsure of how I could provide for my family, let alone chase my dreams.

In my first twenty-five years of life, I traveled the world a grand total of three times. Now I travel the world consistently, every month. Before joining this industry, I didn't think that was going to be possible for me with my record.

I've learned how to set goals and accomplish them with high accuracy. I've learned amazing people skills. I've learned how to mentor other people and set them up for success. Heck, I didn't even read books before April 2015, and now I'm writing them.

~~~

Shortly after I started my business, my mother was diagnosed with stage 4 lung cancer. My mother has always been there for me. She was the one person who was always in my corner no matter what and is the reason I am who I am today. I encouraged her to do a natural treatment, but she decided to go with chemotherapy.

In 2015, she was named Ferguson's Citizen of the Year and was honored in the Fourth of July parade for all that she has done for our community. The Ferguson Youth Initiative has made such a great impact in Ferguson. All my mother wanted was to create something loving that would live on after she left this world.

Stephanie and I decided to get back together shortly after I got home from prison. One night Stephanie and I were at her sister's birthday party, and Stephanie's mother asked me when I was going to marry her daughter. She planted the seed in my head, and it didn't take me long to act on it.

I took my mother with me to design the

ring. My mother gave me her ring that my grandmother had given to her. We used the center stone for the new ring.

I decided I was going to propose to Stephanie in September 2015 while we were in Las Vegas for my company's international convention. This was my first time attending an event like this, so I didn't know how it worked. However, I knew it was a huge event, and I wanted to make it as memorable as possible for Stephanie. I asked our director of distributor relations when would be the best time for me to propose, and she asked me if I wanted to do it onstage at the MGM Grand in front of over five thousand people. I accepted the offer.

I have never felt more nervous in my life. I wasn't afraid of speaking in front of all those people. I was afraid that she might say no in front of all those people. Stephanie didn't have a clue of what I had planned. She said yes, of course, and I felt the weight of the world leave my shoulders. It was an amazing experience.

Stephanie's mother got really sick right before we left for Vegas, which ended up being cancer. A little over a week after we got home, she passed away. That was really hard on Stephanie, her family, and on me. Her mother was a very sweet woman who loved her family dearly. I am forever grateful for her positive influence in my life.

Then my business started to fall apart. Most of the people who had joined quit on themselves. Eventually everyone gave up except one guy. John stayed with it and is still with me to this day. This business isn't for everyone. It takes a rare breed: someone with a lot of resilience, someone who doesn't quit.

My mother's condition was getting worse. In November 2015, she was no longer able to take care of herself, so we had her move in with Stephanie and me. On December 14, 2015, my mother passed away. I was heartbroken, but I was prepared for it. Everything that happened leading up to my mother's death prepared me for it. I will forever love that woman and be grateful for the love she gave me and how she raised me. I have never met anyone with as much love to give as she had. Her legacy carries on through me and all of the people she impacted.

Stephanie and I got married April 2, 2016. It was a beautiful wedding, and I am so grateful I have an amazing wife. She keeps our home tight together and always makes sure her family is taken care of. Especially at dinnertime.

Today I have multiple sources of income. I work from the comfort of my home and enjoy my time freedom. I have insanely huge, gigantic goals and dreams, including writing this book. I set most of these goals and dreams when I first started my business in November 2014. I have a long way to go, but I am well on my way to achieving each one because of my drive and my mind-set. Quite frankly, I just don't quit.

I made a complete turnaround, and I am so grateful that my mother got to see me turn my life around and got to meet her grandsons before she passed.

If I can go from where I was in life to where I am now, then it is never too late for you to accomplish your dreams and get to where you need to be. The only way that you can lose is to give up, not to try.

In the following chapters, I am going to share with you what it took for me to make this transformation and how you can reach the promised land. I am going to break it down into five simple steps that you can apply to your life.

Chapter 5
Step 1: Control Your Thoughts and Guard Your Mind

Before you can change anything in your life, you must first learn to change the way you think. You must learn to control your thoughts and guard your mind. What do I mean by that? You must train your mind to think positive thoughts and envision positive outcomes to every situation, and you must guard your mind from all external negative factors such as other people, TV, music, and so on.

Our subconscious mind is more powerful than we can imagine. Understand that we do possess a second hidden mind that functions day and night beyond the awareness of our conscious mind. Understanding and working with your subconscious mind is the basis of all mind-power techniques. It is the key to your happiness and success.

Individuals who live their life without an understanding and working relationship with their own personal subconscious—and this is the vast majority of the population—limit themselves immeasurably. It is unfortunate because it is not difficult to establish a functioning relationship with your subconscious mind.

Our subconscious mind is like a command center. It acts and attracts what it is commanded to do daily. Its one and only weakness is that it doesn't know true from false, yes or no. It just acts on anything put into our conscious mind. This is why it is so important to feed your mind with positive, loving, and abundant thoughts and to guard your mind from destructive thoughts.

A good example is reading good literature. By reading powerful books such as *As a Man Thinketh* by James Allen or *Think and Grow Rich* by Napoleon Hill, we are feeding our subconscious mind powerful thoughts, which then alter our beliefs in ourselves in a positive way—which then follow into our actions. We then become happier and more successful.

Never tell yourself "I can't" or even say the words "I can't." That is an affirmation, and by thinking or saying it, you are giving it power and attracting that result into your life. Instead of thinking or saying "I can't," say or think "How can I?" Thinking and saying "I can't" commands the subconscious mind to shut down and believe it can't. When we think or say "How can I?" it commands our subconscious mind to tap into its creative sources for a solution.

We also need to be cautious of the time we spend sitting in front of our televisions. Remember, our subconscious mind picks up on anything it is fed, whether it is good or bad, right or wrong. Can you think of anything on TV that you wouldn't want your subconscious mind picking up on? How about your kids, if you have any?

Let me throw this at you. Take a look at the news. It's almost like it is designed to instill fear and hate into its viewers. It is full of stories of war, hate, poverty, hunger, and disease. It is programmed to come on first thing in the morning, so we start our day feeding our subconscious mind with fear and hate, and it is programmed to come on again at night, so we go to bed with that same fear and hate.

We become what we think about the most. Visualization is very powerful. When I first went to prison, I visualized myself getting in amazing physical shape and covered in tattoos. I would think about this and visualize it all day long. Sure enough, that's exactly what happened. When I went back to prison, I visualized myself turning my life around, being with my family, and being successful. We become what dominates our thoughts. Everything man has created in this world has started as a thought and a dream.

Don't focus on what you don't want because you are giving it power and energy, and you are attracting it into your life. Instead, focus on what you want and what you want to become.

I used to think that I was doomed to have bad luck and that everything that could go wrong would go wrong for me. I was a victim. That kind of thinking led me to prison.

When my sister passed away, I changed my thinking. I began to tell myself constantly that I was not going to be like everyone around me, in and out of prison for the rest of my life. I did well for a while, but I didn't discipline my thoughts. Eventually, I fell back into negative thinking.

When I woke up in jail twenty days before my sons were born, I made the decision to own up to everything and take full responsibility for every single thing that happened in my life, whether good or bad. I committed to disciplined thinking. I realized things didn't happen *to* me; things happened *because* of me.

No more crybaby, whining, victim role. One of my favorite role models, Grant Cardone, said in his book *The 10X Rule*, "Anyone who uses blame as the reason why something happened or did not happen will never accumulate real success in life and only further his or her status as a slave on this planet." Wow!

Have you ever noticed that the people who are always whining, complaining, blaming, and making excuses never move forward in life? They are either moving backward or are at a standstill.

The first step in success is to realize we, by our thoughts, create every single circumstance in our lives. We are in complete control. Whether you think you can or can't, you're right. I used to think I couldn't figure out technology and phones, and I was right until someone showed me I could. I started believing I could. Now I can do all kinds of cool stuff with my phone when at one point, I couldn't even figure out how to make a phone call with it.

Last, I want to touch on positive affirmations and the power of using the words "I am" instead of "I will" or "I want." Saying positive affirmations every day with conviction and emotion behind them commands the subconscious mind to attract these affirmations into your life.

A huge reason why I have the confidence I do and why I don't give up is because my mother told me positive affirmations every day. She said to me every day, "You can do anything you put your mind to." She fed my subconscious mind every day to know anything is possible. It is programmed in me to this day.

By using the power of "I am," you are proclaiming it as already done in your life, therefore commanding your subconscious mind to act as if it already is. I'm not saying that you say, "I am a millionaire," and it will happen overnight. I am telling you that if you use the power of "I am" every day over time, if you believe it 100 percent and take action, that it works.

Chapter 6
Step 2: Surround Yourself with Winners

One of my favorite quotes by the great Les Brown is, "If you hang out with nine losers, you're about to become number ten." Brilliant. Jim Rohn states, "You're the average of the five people you come into contact with the most." My mother always told me, "Birds of a feather flock together."

When I was hanging out with drug addicts, I became a drug addict. When I was hanging out with losers, I was a loser. When I associated with scumbags, I acted like a scumbag. Simple as that. I can look at every single phase of my life, and I clearly became just like the company I kept.

I quit hanging out with, I'd say, 95 percent of the people I knew before getting out of prison the final time. Once I surrounded myself with motivated, loving, driven, ambitious, and successful people, that was exactly what I became. When you start hanging out with successful people, you start to pick up their daily habits that got them where they are now and are taking them even further on the road to success.

It is critical that you get rid of any poisonous people in your life if you want to be happy. If they don't have your best interest at heart, if they tell you that you can't do something, if they laugh at you for having dreams and going after them, if they say things to put you down, then they are not your friends. You need to remove them from your circle if you want to have true success and happiness in your life. It's just like guarding your mind. It's hard to stay positive and focused on your dreams and goals when you choose to hang out with people who tell you "you can't" all the time, are constantly laughing at you for going after your dreams, or influence you to participate in something that goes against your dreams and beliefs.

A real friend is always going to have your back and will always encourage you to go after your dreams. A real friend doesn't tell you what you want to hear. A real friend tells you what you *need* to hear.

Energy is contagious, good or bad. Have you ever heard someone say, "I got a bad vibe from him," or "I felt so much energy just being around that group"? That's because we feed off the energy in our surroundings.

So if you are around people who whine, make excuses, have a bad outlook on life, and are not striving to become better, that energy is going to rub off on you. They put a damper on your day just by spending time with you.

However, if you are around a group of extremely excited individuals who are passionate about their dreams, it is almost impossible not to feed off their energy.

When you surround yourself with other individuals who have the same or similar dreams as you and are equally or even more passionate and enthusiastic about their dreams and life, something magical happens. When you have people in your life who encourage you every day to go after your dreams and tell you when they think you are not giving it 100 percent of your effort, it makes the process of attaining your dreams possible and inspires you to persevere. We all need encouragement to take on big goals, and we definitely all need someone to hold us accountable by letting us know when we are getting off-track from our goals.

If you want to live a happy and successful life, start eliminating negative people from your life completely and start surrounding yourself with people whom you want to be like. Watch how much of a difference it will make in your life when you surround yourself with winners.

Chapter 7
Step 3: Replace Bad Habits with Good Ones

Humans are creatures of habit. A habit is a routine of behavior that is repeated regularly and tends to occur subconsciously. Charles Duhigg, reporter for the *New York Times* and author of *The Power Of Habit*, said, "About 40 percent to 45 percent of what we do every day sort of feels like a decision, but it's actually habit." Even the smartest, most creative, most ruggedly individualistic of *Homo sapiens* are on autopilot much of the time, eating, working, and communicating with others through habit.

There are some good evolutionary

reasons for this: habits save us time and mental energy in negotiating the world and free our minds to invent things like fire and computers. They also limit the size of our brains (and therefore our heads), making it easier for human mothers to survive giving birth. But our hardwired ability to form habits makes us vulnerable, quickly picking up self-destructive patterns, too.

The process by which new behaviors become automatic is called habit formation. Old habits are hard to break, and new habits are hard to form because the behavioral patterns we repeat are imprinted in our neural pathways. But it is possible to form new habits through repetition.

I don't care who you are or what you have accomplished. We all have bad habits to some degree or another. Nobody is perfect. What we need to focus on, then, is analyzing ourselves daily to find bad habits and replace them with good habits.

Many techniques exist for removing established habits like withdrawal of reinforcement by identifying and removing factors that trigger and reinforce the habit. Recognizing and eliminating bad habits as soon as possible is advised. Habit elimination becomes more difficult with age because repetitions reinforce habits cumulatively over a lifetime.

According to Charles Duhigg, there is a loop that includes a cue, a routine, and a reward for every habit. An example of a habit loop is this: when a TV program ends (cue), you go to the refrigerator (routine) and eat a snack (reward). The key to changing habits is to identify your cue and modify your routine and reward.

For whatever you consider a bad habit, there is a good habit that can replace it. I used to watch TV. I don't like that it consumes a lot of my time, resulting in me being unproductive, and I definitely don't like the way it makes me feel. After watching programs such as the news, *SportsCenter*, or even commercials, I would have worry, fear, anger, or even feelings of hate flowing through me, and those are feelings I want to avoid at all costs. This also goes with protecting your mind from anything harmful. I started replacing TV with books that enlighten my mind, body, and soul, thanks to my mentor Marlene who wouldn't stop encouraging me to read, do some physical activity like exercising, or conversing with other people. Now I don't watch TV except when the Los Angeles Rams are playing.

Identify the habits you want to change, then identify the cue and modify the routine and reward. And if you fail on your initial attempts, don't give up. Figure out what went wrong and plan strategies to overcome that obstacle the next time. Keep your positive attitude and keep trying. You will get it eventually.

Chapter 8
Step 4: Get Comfortable with Being Uncomfortable

The ability to take a risk by stepping outside of our comfort zone is the primary way by which we grow. But we are often afraid to take that first step. In all reality, comfort zones are not really about comfort; they are about fear. Break the chains of fear to get outside that zone. Once you do, you will learn to enjoy the process of taking risks and growing in the process. Mark Twain said, "Do what you fear the most, and the death of fear is certain."

Stepping outside of your comfort zone is an absolutely necessary factor in personal growth. How can we evolve in our lives and our careers if we only stick to habit and routine?

Failure is not a bad thing. In fact, failure is part of the learning process. It shapes us and defines our character. We must fail over and over again in order to attain new levels of success. Remember, success is overcoming a challenge. Therefore, you can't succeed without facing some kind of difficulty. Reaching new heights involves the risk of attempting something outside of our comfort zone that we may not succeed at on the first few attempts. Take risks.

Let me ask you this: Were you able to talk and put together full, comprehendible sentences the moment you were born? No. It took years of failed attempts at communicating with other human beings before you were able to speak full sentences that others could understand. You had to fail over and over again until you were successful. It is no different with things we haven't done before.

The fear of failure can be almost paralyzing to the ability to take action at times, which is why it is so important to get in the habit of getting out of your comfort zone and to become comfortable with being uncomfortable. John Gardner wrote in the book *Self-Renewal*, "We pay a heavy price for our fear of failure. It is a powerful obstacle to growth. It assures the progressive narrowing of the personality and prevents exploration and experimentation. There is no learning without some difficulty and fumbling. If you want to keep on learning, you must keep on risking failure—all your life."

One of the best ways to conquer a fear is to act on it immediately. Do not give it time to grow by trying to strategize and prepare for it; just take it head on. Grant Cardone also wrote in his book *The 10X Rule*, "The more time you devote to the object of your apprehension, the stronger it becomes. So starve the fear of its favorite food by removing time from its menu." By acting on our fears immediately, we don't allow it time to grow and become more difficult to face.

When we get into the habit of getting comfortable with being uncomfortable, we begin to conquer our fears. This doesn't happen just by doing it one time. Joe Morton said it best in his book *Positive In*, "When we take action, when we 'do,' there is something that happens within us that changes our fear to courage." He also went on to say, "Just by consistently 'doing' you will overcome your fears. Notice how I said consistently. It is not just doing something once. Like a muscle, you need to practice to get stronger over time. It is a process and you will get better at it."

To become more, expand your comfort

zone and get comfortable with being uncomfortable. Learn to look for fear and use it as an indicator of the very thing that you need to do next. Act on it immediately. Fear is the best indicator to determine which actions will provide the greatest return. Become a lion and face your fears.

Chapter 9
Step 5: Stop Making Excuses

I'd like to start this final chapter by saying excuses suck. Excuses are for people who refuse to take responsibility for their life and their circumstances. Excuses get you nowhere in life. The dictionary defines it as "to try to remove blame from." So an excuse is just a justification for doing—or not doing—something. How many goals have you achieved in life by making excuses? Better yet, how many goals have you not even attempted to achieve because you made excuses not to?

If there is something that you want, you have to commit to it, all in, and you cannot make any excuses as you move toward that goal if you have any hopes of attaining it. Grant Cardone said in *The 10X Rule*, "No excuse exists that can or will make you successful. Engaging in self-pity and excuse-making are signs that someone has an extremely minimal degree of responsibility."

When I was fired from my sales job at the clothing store, I acted like a crybaby and started whining, throwing a pity party, and made excuses to party and drink because of it. Did that help me achieve my goal of having a successful career and money in my pockets? No, it put me in worse circumstances. It actually cost me money and time during my life in prison that I will never get back. Excuses suck.

Do you like being powerless? Of course you don't like being powerless. No one does. Yet when you make excuses, you are making false claims by saying the reason why you did or didn't do something was because of some external factor other than yourself, and therefore, you are proclaiming that you are powerless over your very own actions.

By taking responsibility for every action and inaction in our lives, we can then learn from them and grow. We then begin to make progress toward our goals and dreams.

Don't make excuses. Make it happen.

Conclusion

I hope after reading this book, you come away inspired to go after your dreams like your life depends on it—because it does. You're doing one of two things in your lifetime, either building your dream or building someone else's dream. We all have our very own purpose in life, and we were not put on this earth to conform to how other people say we should live our lives. If you are not doing what your heart desires and what you truly love, then you are not living.

Whatever your current circumstance is right now, it doesn't have to be a hopeless situation. It is hopeless only if you allow it to be. You are in complete control of your life moving forward, no matter what circumstance you are in at this very moment. Your past does not determine your future. It's your choice how you shape and mold the outcome.

As my mother told me every day, "You can do anything you put your mind to." If you learn to control your thoughts and guard your mind, surround yourself with winners, replace bad habits with good ones, get comfortable with being uncomfortable, and make no excuses, then you can have, do, and be anything your heart desires.

It all starts with a decision and taking immediate action. You, my friend, are greatness. Now go show the world that it isn't over until we die.

Follow Zachary on Social Media!

WinWithZach

@winwithzach

@winwithzach

@zacctbabcock

Zachary Babcock